Creative
With Friends
Times

Creative
With Friends
Times

Doug Fields & Todd Temple

Illustrations by Steve Björkman

OLIVER
NELSON

A Division of Thomas Nelson Publishers
Nashville

Published in Nashville, Tennessee, by Oliver-Nelson Books, a division of Thomas Nelson, Inc., Publishers, and distributed in Canada by Lawson Falle, Ltd., Cambridge, Ontario.

Printed in the United States of America.

ISBN 0-8407-9560-2

Library of Congress Cataloging-in-Publication Data

Fields, Doug, 1962–
    Creative times with friends.

    1. Friendship—Humor. 2. Friendship—Caricatures
and cartoons. 3. American wit and humor, Pictorial.
I. Temple, Todd, 1958–   . II. Title.
PN6162.F47 1988   818'.5402   88–29015
ISBN 0-8407-9560-2 (pbk.)

1 2 3 4 5 6 — 93 92 91 90 89 88

Contents

1.

Communication

Superficial Talk Among Friends

Hi—how are you?"
"Fine—how are you?"
"I'm doing good, thanks."
"So, what's new with you?"
"Nothing much—how about you?"
"Not much—just trying to keep busy."
"Yeah, me too."
"Yeah? So what have you been doing?"

...COOL...
50's

...GROOVY...
60's

...FAR OUT....
70's

...TOTALLY...
80's

..COOL..
90's

"Oh, same ol', same ol'."
"Yeah, me too."
"Who are you rooting for in the World Series?"
"It doesn't matter to me—I'm not much of a baseball fan."

"Yeah, I'd just like to see a good series."
"Sure is nice weather for a game."
"You're not kidding—the weather's been great."
"It sure is nice to have a little sun these days."
Another person enters conversation. "Hi, Tim—how are you?"
"Let me introduce you to my good friend, Mark."
"Hi—nice to meet you."
"Thanks. So what do you do?"

Superficial Talk Among Meaningless Minds

"Hi—how are you?"
"Fine, thanks. Who stole the cookie from the cookie jar?"
"Where did you get that armored car in your hat?"
"That's what you think, Mom. Are the dishes clean?"
"Why are you talking about stuffed animals when it's raining outside?"
"I've been there even before it had people."

"If it's okay with you, it's okay with me."

"I'm hungry. What's playing at the movies?"

"It's nice to meet you. My name is Tom."

"I'll be right back—I have to go to the bathroom before I can go skating."

"I'm a Republican who loves traffic."

Meaningless Talk Among Superficial Teenagers

"Well, like, how are you?"

"Hi—like, how are you?"

"Totally bummed. It's so lame I can't even believe it."

"What's so wrong that's got you, like, stressed?"

"Randy . . . he's just so . . . so, like, rude to me and I mean, I didn't do anything to him, I swear."

"I can totally relate. Duane said to me, 'It's over,' and I said, 'So what—you're so lame I can't even believe I, like, went with you.'"

"Just because I, like, waved to my stupid sixth-grade boyfriend. Oh my gosh, Randy, he, like, like, almost totally trashed me. I said, 'What?' Then he said, well, he didn't really, like, say anything, but . . . I was so totally scared. He, like, shook his head and walked away. Can you, like, *even* believe he did that? He, like, *totally* blew me off."

"Me too! Guys are so, like . . . ooohhh . . . dumb. I'll, like, catch ya later."

"See ya, like, maybe later?"

Conversation Jump Starts

The conversation lulls and you stare at your knee. *What can we talk about? What will I say next?* The next time you're in this situation, just pull out one of these sure-fire jump starters—you'll have the words flowing again in a flash.

- Tell him your worst sin, and ask him to tell you his.
- Begin, "Knock knock . . ."

- Ask, "Why do you hate me?"
- Say, "People tell me you'd like a sex change . . ."

- Ask, "Why haven't you ever been able to make much of yourself?"

Decision-Making Helps

If the following dialogue sounds familiar, you need some decision-making helps: "I don't care. What do you want to do?" "It makes no difference to me. Why don't you decide tonight?" Next time you hit this famous stalemate, you might try one of these techniques (the losing partner should make the decision).

- Flip a coin.
- Play rock-paper-scissors.
- Race up the stairs.
- See who can spit farther.

- Add your height to your age, subtract your shoe size, and then multiply by the number of freckles you have on your left cheek.

- See who can make the grosser sound with his armpit.
- See who can scream louder.
- Throw glass jars against a wall and decide (by counting) whose jar broke into more pieces.
- See who can jam more small marshmallows up his nose.
- Pour vinegar over open flesh wounds—the first to scream loses.
- See who can keep his hand in the snake cage longer—the first to get bitten loses.
- Back a car tire over your feet—the first to scream loses.
- Scratch a chalkboard with your fingernails—the first to plug her ears loses.
- See who can watch "General Hospital" longer without laughing at the acting.
- See who can go longer without blinking.
- See who can stick his tongue in the light socket longer.
- Play Motley Crue at full volume—the first to blow his eardrums loses.

Looking Out for a Friend

You know someone's a friend when she takes the time to prevent your embarrassment (like when you have something hanging from your nose and she signals you before anyone else notices). In fact, most friends have an arsenal of techniques they use to protect each other. Here are a few of the internationally recognized gestures for helping a friend avoid embarrassment.

"There's a foreign object on the end of your nose."

"Your body odor is noticeable."

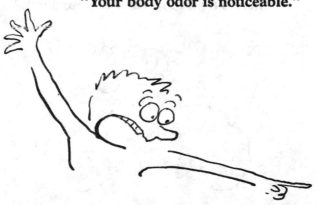

"Your zipper is down."

"Your slip is showing."

"There's a piece of food in your teeth."

"You said something derogatory about my mother."

**"A large piano has been dropped from
the 125th-story window, and you're
about to become an E chord."**

"Your shirt is misbuttoned."

"You're using bad language."

"A train is about to run you over."

MINUTES PER DAY WE COMMUNICATE
WITH OUR WORLD*

Strangers in traffic	43
Business associates	31
Air	18
Strangers in general	12
Spouse	11
Child	7
Dog	6
Friends	5
Plants	4
Wrong numbers	1

*This information was compiled by the research department of Genoway, Nevins, and Johnson.**

Actually, it's not a legitimate research department. To be honest, Jeff Genoway is a fireman, Chris Nevins lives in Palm Desert, and Russ Johnson is Todd's brother-in-law. But they're all great guys and good friends, and that's what this book is all about, isn't it?*

Well, the book is really about friends in general and makes no particular mention of anything to do with great guys. The above statistics (excluding everything but the figures for "spouse" and "child") were heard by a popular speaker at a convention we went to last year. The rest of the stuff we made up while eating french fries and drinking iced tea at Carl's Jr.*

****We apologize that the name of the speaker can't be mentioned. He really wasn't supposed to be at the convention, and we don't want to get him in trouble with anyone in his family. His family may not care, though, because they probably don't talk more than 11 minutes a day.*****

*****We don't know, but it may be more or less than 11 minutes because the above statistics aren't really true. They're for entertainment only.******

******This won't apply to you if you weren't entertained.*******

*******Shame on you.

PSSST! I DRAW THE PICTURES FOR THIS BOOK AND YOU READERS SHOULD KNOW THAT THE WRITERS ARE REALLY WEIRD.

(I'M NOT KIDDING)

How to Inform a Friend He Has Bad Breath

- Breathe into his face and say, "That's what I go through every time we talk."
- Stick two tubes of nasal spray up your nose.
- Ask, "Did we drive past a freshly fertilized field or do you need some mouthwash?"

THAT BAD, HUH?

- Squint and make your eyes water when you're listening to him speak.
- Ask, "Could you eat nothing but peppermint whenever we're together?"
- Say, "Hanging around you is making me begin to believe in dragons."

UH, CINDY... BEFORE WE GO ON WITH THIS CONVERSATION...UH...UM... COULD YOU PLEASE TAKE A BREATH MINT?

Talking to Strangers

You're waiting for your flight in the gate area of an airport. Seated across from you is a friendly looking gentleman who seems eager to start up a conversation. But you're at the climax in your book (the main character is standing at the top of treacherous slope, bucket of water in hand; his sister is asking him to come down). Should you put down the book and make conversation or finish the chapter? Out of the corner of your eye, you see a book on corporate mergers in his open briefcase. Is it a coincidence that the author's initials match those on the edge of the briefcase?

Lowering your book just far enough to survey him secretly, you observe his tailored suit and Rolex watch. His demeanor exudes confidence. *He* must *be the president and major stockholder of a billion-dollar company. And if I start talking to him, he might offer me a job, possibly a vice-presidency in the company—which would be slightly better than the graveyard shift I've been pulling at the koi-fish breeding farm.*

He looks like he's in his fifties, which means that if he got married straight out of college, and if he had a daughter within the first few years of marriage, she's probably about thirty, possibly unmarried, and most likely extremely beautiful. And once I got the job, I might meet her sometime when she stopped by the office to pick up the keys to the corporate jet for a skiing weekend in Alberta. And if I were ever invited to join the family for weekends at the "cottage" on Canandaigua Lake, I might accompany her on evening strolls after talking business with her father. On one of those strolls, I might ask her to marry me, and then her father might want to keep control of the company inside the family by making me president when he retires. You decide to put down your book and speak with him.

But wait. What's that lump in his coat? *Probably a thick wad of hundred-dollar bills. Or maybe it's a pistol. How could he get a pistol through the metal detector? A man as sharp and successful as he is could figure out a way. But maybe he's not a success. Maybe he's not even the president of a billion-dollar company. Maybe he's a terrorist* posing *as the president of a billion-dollar company. The suit, the watch, the briefcase, the book—all of it might be part of his costume. The book's pages might be carved out to conceal a secret weapon—or a plastic explosive. He might be the perpetrator of a plot to hijack the plane to Minnewaukan, North Dakota. Maybe he's smiling at me because he's just realized that I'm taller than he is, and he can use me as a human shield in the fusillade that would erupt if the FBI should discover him before boarding. If I start talking to him, I could listen carefully for a strange accent—that would confirm my suspicion. But others might see us talking together, and they'd testify that I was friendly with him, and probably his accomplice. And if I were charged with aiding a terrorist, I might drive myself mad in the jail cell while awaiting justice (oh, why do its wheels turn so slowly?), and in my deranged state I might convince myself that the reason why all this is happening to me is that when I was seven I put rabbit pellets in my little brother's Cocoa Puffs, and I'm finally getting what I have long deserved. And I might be sentenced to life in prison with no possibility of parole, and the days would creep by, month after month, year after year, until I might lose track of* "Time?"

"Yes—do you have the time? My watch seems to have stopped." *He's talking to me!*

"It's 3:30."

"Thank you."

No accent. Cheap watch. Well, no bother— there's always your book. It's safer than talking to strangers.

Friendly Gestures

To the foreigner traveling in the United States, our social customs and gestures can be very confusing: behavior that is taboo in his culture is perfectly acceptable here; behavior he considers polite is rude or even dangerous here.

If you're a foreigner with a sincere desire to fit in with us natives and follow our customs, we've compiled a list of some friendly gestures you can try. We've also identified some rude gestures that are often confused for the friendly ones because of their similarity. Although the differences are subtle in appearance, they are radically different in meaning.

Situation: At a busy intersection, a policeman directs you through a snarling mess of traffic.

Friendly Gesture: Roll down the window and wave your hand as you drive by.

Rude Gesture: Roll down the window and rub his bald spot as you drive by.

Situation: In the supermarket, a well dressed woman walks past you and smiles.
Friendly Gesture: Nod and tip your hat.
Rude Gesture: Nod and tip her cart.

Situation: You're walking through the mall and see an old friend.
Friendly Gesture: Offer him your hand.
Rude Gesture: Offer him your nose.

Situation: A child accidentally drops a handful of change onto the floor.
Friendly Gesture: Pick up the money and hand it back to him.
Rude Gesture: Pick up the money and run.

Situation: As you enter a revolving door, a woman on the other side gets her purse strap caught.
Friendly Gesture: Stop pushing the door and wait until she frees the strap.
Rude Gesture: Press on the door until the purse is launched through the other side.

Situation: A gust of wind sweeps a man's umbrella out of his hands and carries it down the street.
Friendly Gesture: Chase down the umbrella and return it to its owner.
Dangerous Gesture: Get into your car, hunt down the umbrella, and drive over it.

What We Say Isn't Always What We Mean

Fact: We can't read people's minds.
Truth: People don't always verbalize what they are thinking. They don't want to say what's on their minds—especially when they are asked ridiculous questions. These "disguised" feelings are communicated with appeasing answers. Here are a few snappy responses to stupid questions.

Situation #1

Tim just crashed his parents' car. It's totaled. He wasn't supposed to be driving while they were out of town—especially their Mercedes.

Question asked: "Hey, Tim, sorry to hear about the accident—are you bummed?"
Question answered: "Ah, it's no big deal."
What should have been said: "Are you kidding? I'm thrilled. I wish I could destroy family property on a daily basis. I look forward to the screaming, tears, and punishment that I'll receive when my parents return. You can come over if you'd like—it's going to be great. Hey, can I drive your car for a few minutes?"

Situation #2

Carol has been working at home all day. The kids have been unmanageable, the tub has overflowed, the phone has been ringing off the hook, and Fido was hit

by a car. Carol's husband, Jack, comes home and notices dinner isn't ready.

Question asked: "Carol, where's dinner why isn't it
   ready what have you been doing today?"
Question answered: "It's in the refrigerator. I haven't
   had time to take it out."
What should have been said: "Let me put a dead dog
   around your neck, a mop in your hand, three
   screaming kids in your pockets, and a phone sticking from your ear and see if you have time to make a
   tuna casserole for a lazy husband who thinks being
   a security guard at a waterbed store is stressful
   work."

Situation #3

A newspaper reporter is talking to the losing coach
after a championship game.

Question asked: "Are you disappointed to end your
   season with a loss?"

Question answered: "Not really—the kids played hard. We were just outplayed today."

What should have been said: "No, I enjoy losing big games when the school's reputation and my career are on the line. We practice for nine months, forty hours a week, while surviving injuries and breaking up fights just for the thrill of being asked questions by compassionate and educated people like you."

2.

Outrageous Times with Friends

Get out of the rut! Stop doing the same old thing every time you get together with friends. Try something outrageous for a change.

Shopping with Friends

Friends spend time in grocery stores. You can do crazy things with others that you wouldn't do if alone. Here are a few ideas:

1. Test-drive your shopping cart. Find one in the parking lot (it's already warmed up) and run it full speed, making sure a wheel isn't acting on its own be-

BANZAI ! !

half and turning in circles. After you find a cart that passes the wheel test, your last job is to put a small child in it and run it over a speed bump. If the kid can stay in the cart, you found a winner. If he falls out, keep looking.

2. *Scout the cookies.* On your way in the store, look back at your friend and motion her to hurry up. While your head is facing the parking lot, run your cart into the table filled with Girl Scout cookies. Don't injure an innocent little scout—especially if it was her little brother you used for the speed-bump test. (Of course you'll want to buy at least one box. Thin mints are the best and may come in handy for skipping across the grocery store floor.)

3. *Play "doorman."* Before you enter the store, one person should stand beside the electronic door and step it open as people approach. Bow while waving them in. Once shoppers get inside the store, they should be greeted by a friendly valet waiting with a shopping cart near the turnstile.

4. *Get fresh with the produce.* It's time to begin your shopping fun. Go to the vegetable section and see who can find the largest tomato—use the scale to ensure a real winner. While your friend is looking for his vegetable, hose him down with the lettuce sprayer (be on the lookout if he's read this book). If a third person is involved, the two of you can wrap her in cellophane from head to toe and place her neatly in the frozen-fish section. Try to design people, animals, or farm tractors by combining fruits with vegetables—and be sure to leave them for the delight of future shoppers.

5. *Sort the cereal.* Down the cereal aisle, find the boxes with the least and most sugar. Compare prices, and then buy the one that's worst for you. If there are more than ten cereal types, rearrange them into alphabetical order (this is an old Diponesian secret seldom practiced in the States these days). Check the Wheaties box to see if the person on the front is still alive. (If he's not, that's old cereal—you'd better complain.)

6. Be the "candy man." Good grocery stores have candy sections that allow you to pick and choose and pay by the pound. Bag some candy and give it to the kid who is walking estranged from her mom. Explain how you are giving free candy while promoting products. When she runs to inform her mom, make sure you aren't around to get pointed at. Peek through the bread section and watch how she tries to be convincing with her new gift.

7. Toy with the merchandise. Fill your shopping cart with pet accessories (usually near the toiletries). Take the plastic bones, yarn balls, and squeaking rubber replicas to the toy department. Replace the toys with the pet paraphernalia—then do the same in the pet section. If everyone in the world did this, cats would play with guns while little kids pick yarn from their teeth. (And cat owners would save money in kitty litter!)

8. Confuse the clerk. On your way through the checkout stand, ask the clerk to line your paper bags with plastic. Place your groceries on the scale and ask if you can pay by the pound. Pay in pennies. If the clerk gets mad, ask if she has change for a million.

9. Leave happy. Upon leaving, smile at the manager and thank him for a good time. Wave to the Girl Scout and chase her brother with a shopping cart.

Imaginary Shopping Spree

Take a friend to your favorite store. Imagine that each of you has $1,000 to spend inside the store within the next hour. If the store doesn't sell anything for such a small amount, splurge and make the amount $10,000. The really fun part comes when the game is over and you realize you don't need any of the things you bought. Take your "purchases" to the register and see if you can get a cash refund on the returns.

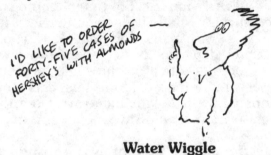

Water Wiggle

Do you remember this toy? You hook it to your hose, and the water pressure raises the serpent from the ground, drenching everyone around as it dances and wanders across the lawn. Set it up in your front yard on a hot day, and then charge admission to adults who want to join in the fun.

Big-Rig Shopping

Some people like to take a Saturday afternoon to test-drive cars. Forget the cars. Go to a truck dealer and test-drive a big rig. If you don't have the proper license, the salesman probably won't let you off the lot, which is okay. If you don't have a license you probably don't know how to drive one of those big-time machines, and you'd be content to just sit in the driver's seat and make engine noises.

The Art of Riding Shotgun

Typically we do the same sorts of things when we are passengers in a car. We put on a seat belt, sit up, and face forward. At times we look for addresses, turn the air vents towards the back, and talk to strangers for directions. Many people don't realize, however, that the true art of riding shotgun is to make the driver laugh, sweat, and swerve into other lanes. If screaming at inappropriate times doesn't work, try some of the following.

- Sit backward.
- Turn on the windshield wipers.
- Blast the radio.
- Put all the preset stations on the same channel.
- Move the passenger seat forward and backward.
- Take the car out of gear at stop signs and lights.

- Put your feet on the dashboard.
- Readjust the rearview mirror.

- Unscrew the knob on the stick shift.
- Pull the emergency brake while the car is in motion.
- Pull out the headrest.
- Put your hands over the driver's eyes.
- Spray paint the inside of the window.
- Tweak the side mirrors.
- Smudge the upholstery.
- Activate the trunk release.
- Throw the contents of the glove box out the window.
- Spit on the window.
- Honk the horn and duck.

Ideas for Groups of One Thousand or More

It's hard enough to think of creative things to do with a few friends. But when you have a thousand or more of your personal friends over for a good time, it's a real challenge. Try these:

Hide and seek. In most neighborhoods you'll run out of hiding places after the first two or three hundred people are hidden. To accommodate the larger group,

expand the boundaries to the city limits. If you live in a small town, make it the county line. If you cannot find a large enough section to play in, simply form teams: each team of fifty must hide together and, of course, tag home base together.

Twister. This favorite of the past takes on a new dimension with any group over one thousand.

Poker. You'll need more than one deck.

Charades. Play it in a stadium. Half of team A sit in the stands while the other half try to spell out the word on the field with their bodies. When their teammates guess correctly, it's time for team B to give it a try.

Balloon Pong

By combining the art of Ping-Pong with the sport of tennis, you and your friend can work up a sweat without leaving the house. Grab tennis rackets and an inflated balloon and find a spacious room. Pound the

I COULDN'T FIND A BALLOON, SO I THOUGHT I'D USE A GOLF BALL.

balloon around and invent your own rules for this slow-motion, Ping-Pong–like game. With the money you'll save by not paying clubhouse dues, replacing tennis balls you hit into the street, and having surgery for your tennis elbow, you can buy some macaroni and cheese and eat like queens.

Fun at the Pool

Pool Toys

Most pools where adults hang out are just plain boring. The adults simply lie there, eating, sweating, and reading novels by people who write even worse than we do. The only adults *in* the pool are those trying to

I KNOW GIRLS, AND I KNOW THEY'LL BE IMPRESSED WITH THIS INFLATABLE POOL TOY.

YEAH, BUT I'M THE ONE WITH RADIO-CONTROLLED LEECHES!

drown the mob of fourth graders who have been shouting "Marco?" . . . "Polo!" for the past two and a half hours.

Why is this? *Because there are no pool toys!* Add a few inflatable sea serpents, alligators, and floating cows, and you'll see adults playing in the pool as they should. Go to the toy store, pick up as many inflatable toys as you can afford, and take them to the pool. To avoid passing out, get others to help you inflate them. Once the adults are happily floating and splashing on their plastic vessels, organize a couple of pool-toy games.

Cruise Ships Too Close to the Glacier. One edge of the pool is the glacier, several of the heavier bathers are glacial chunks, and the rest of the floaters are cruise ships. When the cruise ships get too close to the glacier, a few of the glacial chunks break off and fall into the water in front of the ships. The object is for the chunks to land near the cruise ships and cause waves that capsize the floaters.

Pod of Killer Whales Meets Family of Defenseless Seals. In this game, the women (killer whales) line up at one end of the pool; the men (defenseless seals) float on the pool toys in the middle. The object is for the

whales to swim underwater from one end of the pool to the other, overturning as many seals as possible along the way. If a whale takes a breath before reaching the other end of the pool, she's captured and sent to Sea World until she learns how to follow directions.

Marco Polo

Another childhood game making a comeback at some of the finer swim clubs, Marco Polo is the ideal pool game for combining fun, exercise, and practice in cheating. One person is "it," and he tries to tag another person. Since his eyes are closed, he must use a

primitive form of echo location to find his prey: he calls out, "Marco?" and listens for the others to cry out, "Polo!" If he tags someone, that person becomes "it."

Now that you know the rules, here's how to break them:

1. Crawl out of the pool and watch "it" swim in circles trying to find you. (If he calls, "Fish out of water," you're busted.)
2. If you're "it," peek.
3. Swim behind someone who is trying to sneak past "it"; when the victim gets within arm's length of "it," scream, "Polo!"
4. Climb out of the pool and throw in a bucketful of piranha.

Jump or Dive

For the unfortunate souls who missed this when they were younger, here's how you play: One person leaps off the diving board, getting as much height as possible. Another person, the caller, stands on the side of the pool and shouts either "Jump!" or "Dive!" The person in the air then has to adjust her trajectory to

hit the water in the manner called for—not an easy
task.

A more challenging version of this game is called
Crash or Burn: the caller shouts out one of these in-
structions, and the airborne player must "crash"
(belly flop) or "burn" (back flop). WARNING: Never play
this version from the high dive or in an empty pool.

Fun at the Beach

Sand Castles

If you're serious about building a sand castle, con-
struct a full-scale model. Beware of small children
whose parents have taken over their own castle
projects and are, therefore, eager to commandeer
someone else's. The best protection from this hazard
is a life-sized moat. For added safety, fill the moat with
sand crabs.

Sunscreen Painting

Tell your friend that you'd be happy to put sunscreen on her back. But instead of spreading it evenly, write a message with the ointment that will show up later as white skin on a red back: try KICK ME, DON'T SPLASH, or DON'T KICK SAND.

Snorkeling

Snorkel beneath a fishing float. (Most have air channels between the flotation units; you can hide under

the float without being detected.) Use an unbent coat hanger to find a dangling fishhook. Give the fisherman a good fight by whipping the hook back and forth, deeper, then shallower, then let him reel you in for a moment, then fight again. Now pull the hook under the float, carefully attach an old boot to it, and let him reel in his prize. If you have several friends with you, have them load other hooks with the other boot and a pair of socks. CAUTION: Don't attempt this stunt with spearfishermen.

Fun in the Surf*

Body Surfing

This is the oldest and easiest form of surfing. Swim fins make it easier to catch waves (they go on your feet), but if you're a good swimmer or have long, flappy feet, you'll be fine without them. It also helps to have a bathing suit you can actually *swim* in without losing it in a wave. Just before the wave breaks, pre-

NOTE: THIS DOESN'T WORK WELL IN SMALLER LAKES.

tend there's a twenty-foot shark on the other side of it—this motivates you to swim vigorously for the shore with head down and feet kicking like mad. If the front of the wave is higher than you, or if the water is shal-

---

*These activities require waves; so if you're sitting on the shore of Hogback Lake, Indiana, skip it.

lower than you are tall, don't try to ride straight in or you may end up sticking straight up.

When you've got this sport licked, try one of these body-surfing stunts:

Wave Calling. The object of the game is to see who can surf the wave farther into shore. The one who beaches himself higher when the water washes out again is the winner on that wave. Each of you takes turns calling the waves to be surfed: the one "calling" the wave tries to fake the other out by pretending to swim for waves but not calling them, and then calling "Wave!" when she takes the wave she wants. The other person tries to catch the called wave, but if he misses it and the caller catches it, the caller wins the wave automatically. If he catches it and the caller misses it, he wins. If both catch it, the winner is the one who goes farther. If both miss it, the caller picks another wave. Switch callers after each wave ridden. CAUTION: Don't play this game if the beach is rocky or you're allergic to sand in your bathing suit.

Surfing Bodies. One of you is the "surfer" (preferably the lighter one), and the other is the "board" (preferably the heavier one). Take off on a wave, and maneuver yourselves so the surfer climbs on the back of the board. Try to stand. (It's possible, especially if the person acting as the board is fat and buoyant.) If the board's back is too slippery, apply surf wax. When you get really good at this, try tandem surfing, where two of you ride the board, doing various gymnastic stunts before sinking. PLEASE NOTE: You may see advanced body surfers riding waves on their backs—don't try this if you're the board in this game.

Barrel Rolling. Take off on a wave and turn over onto your back. Now continue around onto your front again. Repeat this as many times as you can in the wave until you get seasick.

Lip Launch. This is popular using a surfboard, but

it's also fun using just your body as the missile. The moment a wave begins to break, the top curls over and forms a lip. Swim toward the wave and dive into it just below the lip. The force of the water flowing up the face of the wave will launch you through the top and into the air on the other side. After you get good, take turns going for height, distance, and style. Be sure to keep an eye out for other surfers, jellyfish, and oil tankers.

Body Boarding

The best kinds of body boards are the small foam ones that look like overgrown kick boards. At any crowded ocean beach you'll generally find dozens of these boards in the waves. If you come down the face of a wave on a body board and discover that the water ahead of you is littered with swimmers, pretend you're in the giant slalom and the swimmers are merely gates you must maneuver through. If it looks like you're going to miss a gate, just scream—the "gate" will probably duck underwater and out of harm's way (lift your feet as you go by).

AN INTERESTING NOTE: While it's been reported that sharks are attracted to these synthetic boards—using them as a sort of chewing gum—we've found that they much prefer more "natural" foods.

Skim Boarding

Skim boards are made out of plywood, plastic, or fiberglass. To ride one, throw it onto the thin sheet of water running off the edge of the beach after a wave, run up to it, and jump on firmly with *both* feet. If you try to step on it one foot at a time, you'll do the splits

the instant you touch the board. Skim boards don't glide well if the sand is interrupted by rocks or beached whales.

Surfing

There's something about the sport of surfing that attracts a disproportionate amount of our nation's socially inept. It seems that virtually every kindergartner who was absent during Manners Week grows up and takes up surfing. Well, such phenomena are better left for graduate students to write dissertations on; what matters is that you and your friends can still enjoy surfing *and* teach naughty surfers to be nicer citizens.

Naughty surfers believe they've somehow inherited the beach for their private use and must defend it against all uncool people. When you arrive at the beach with your boards, they may say things like, "Go home, tourist," "Hey, locals only," or "Go back to Kansas!" If they do, reply, "Is your name God?" Be sure to wear nerdy clothes and say goofy things you heard on *Beach Blanket Bingo:* "Cowabunga," "Go daddy go," and "Hot dog!" This will embarrass and disgust the naughty surfers (nerdiness is to naughty surfers what kryptonite is to Superman) so badly that they'll have to clear out before what you have rubs off on them.

HEY, DUDES! THIS IS REALLY SUPER GROOVY!

Naughty surfers think fun is only fun if it makes someone else miserable. So they try to steal every wave you take off on, and aim for you when you get within a furlong of their path. If a naughty surfer steals a wave from you, make him sit in the kelp until he thinks he can act like a good boy. If he does it again, send him to the lifeguard tower. But if he uses his board in a threatening manner, confiscate it until he promises to use it responsibly.

Silly Parties

Sure, you can go to one more party where you sit around and wish you were having as much fun as everyone else is pretending to have. Or you can host a *silly party*. A silly party is any party that causes your guests to do things they'd never do—not because those things would be improper, immoral, or dangerous, but because, well, most people never thought of them before. Here are some ideas:

Mobile Party

This is actually a variation on a popular date from our book *Creative Dating*. Rent a large you-drive truck, fill it with all the comforts of home—couches, tables, chairs, stereo, miniature spoon collection. Drive to your guests' houses, load them into the back, and drive to your favorite back road or secluded parking lot for a party. Unless your sofa is equipped with seat belts, take it easy on corners, speed bumps, and jumps.

Plant Party

Each of the guests comes dressed in plant materials. Like the Rose Parade float competition, judging will be based on the prettiest, most original, most colorful, and so on. Be sure to serve a vegetarian meal—and inform your guests that they may not snack on their costumes.

Rainbow Party

Guests must come dressed in the color they were assigned on their invitations. Everything they're wearing must match the color, and those arriving "out-of-color" are ushered into the backyard where a team of "color costumers" properly coordinate their outfits. Of course, that means pouring tempera paint all over their clothes, and so it's a good idea to make this an *outdoor* rainbow party.

When it's time for dinner, everyone must eat in the order of the rainbow: red foods first, then orange, yellow, green, blue, and purple. Color-blind people can snack between courses. After dinner, pass out squirt guns with colored dye: girls get red dye, guys get blue. Mark the boundaries, and blow a whistle; at the end of five minutes the winners are the ones who have the least amount of enemy color on them. The losers do the dishes.

Servant's Party

This is very much like your normal party, except you aren't allowed to put food in your own mouth. If you want something to eat, you've got to ask someone to feed it to you; if you care for a drink, someone else must pour. If you catch someone cheating, the offender must eat ten Twinkies in front of everyone.

WHO'S GOT THE KETCHUP?

Medical Party

This is best done if you, or someone you know, have connections with a hospital and can get the props you need. Your guests must wear hospital greens and surgical gloves. Serve the food in divided trays, and eat with surgical instruments.

How to Cruise

People fail to realize that cruising is an art. One doesn't simply jump in a car and begin to cruise. We have discovered several cruising techniques while surveying popular cruising spots throughout the United States and Mexico (Pete's Whistle Stop in Tahachapei, California, Sputnik Donut House in Bedford, Pennsylvania, Gopher Hill Theaters in Ridgeland, South Carolina, and Independencia Supermercado in Mexicali, Mexico, to name a few). Here are some essential cruising tips.

Drive slowly. This is not a given. People who cruise fast are dorks. The significant elements of cruising can't be fully experienced in a fast car. By driving slowly, the cruiser is able to see and be seen by the crowd and his imaginary audience.

Play loud music. If you don't have a powerful stereo, don't cruise with the "big boys." A regulation cruiser stereo has at least 100 watts per channel with eight sets of tri-axial speakers. Cruisers seem to be moving toward cassette tapes and away from radio. The change came when Storke Lee Nortee, the president of Cruise International in Shippensburg, Pennsylvania, was playing a rock-n-roll station that suddenly switched to soft rock. Within a second, Neil Diamond was squealing before Storke's friends. Storke lost his presidency and was laughed off the boulevard. Cruising credibility is lost when you have wood box-speakers in your back window (those went out with Nixon, click-clacks, and the Ford Pinto).

Slowly nod and turn your head. This technique is difficult to master but important. Master cruisers nod their head 5 degrees forward while slowly turning their head approximately 15 degrees to each side. (It's easy to spot rookies as they eagerly turn their head 180 degrees to catch all the sights.)

Nodding has become popular over the last five years. It establishes an I'm-cool-enough-

EVIDENCE OF EARLY ASSYRIAN CRUISING

to-be-checked-out-while-I-check-you-out-so-keep-checking-me-out attitude. Practice these motions before taking them to the street.

Don't smile. If you want to smile, go on a joy-ride. Get your Aunt Lilly and Uncle Bartholomew and go for a scenic drive. Smile all you want, laugh and be joyous, but don't flatter yourself that you are cruising.

Limit the number of your passengers. Most cruisers cruise with two people. Three is acceptable but any more becomes uncomfortable, and the in-car dialogue sounds like a family vacation. You may see a car packed with people, but they're probably jocks acting drunk and dumb.

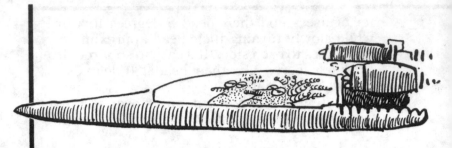

NON-LOCAL CRUISERS

If you choose to cruise with three people, the proper etiquette is as follows:

Three guys	Youngest rides in the back (unless it's his car).
Three girls	Ugliest rides in the back (even if it's her car).
Two guys, one girl	Girl rides in the front if she's dating the driver. If not, she's in the back.
Two girls, one guy	If the guy is the youngest, he's in the back. If he's oldest, he drives. If it's not his car and he can't drive, he should go on a joyride.
Two girls, little brother	Girls ride in the front, little brother rides in the trunk.

Have a clean car. Cruisers are insulted when they see dirty cars. Years ago, if you didn't have mag wheels and pin-striping you were a jerk. Now the same applies to anyone too lazy to wash his car. A clean car is a medallion to the devout cruiser. If you don't want to take the time to keep your car clean, decorate it with paper and balloons and join a parade.

EARLY FARMER GEEZER-CRUISERS

3.

Making a Friend's Day

I'd Vote for You!

Make your friend feel great by giving him your patriotic support. Sign him up to run for President. Start the process by getting his neighbors and colleagues to sign endorsements. Hand him a speech that you've written telling his audience what a great per-

son he is and how he's going to make this world a better place to live. Hang signs that feature his name and face. Set up a voting booth in front of his home or office. When he wins (assuming you want him to), have a victory party with all his supporters.*

Did I Order This?

Periodically, your mail carrier will deliver packets of a hundred 3 x 5 cards advertising various products. The cards are self-addressed and postage-paid for con-

venient and speedy return. Fill out each product card with your friend's address—she'll get junk mail for months to come.

---

*If this works and your friend actually becomes President, we would like you to remember where the idea originated and compensate us accordingly (we won't be holding our breath). Thank you.

Thrift Store Shopping

Create a new wardrobe by searching the thrift store racks. You'll find polyester pants in every color on the color wheel; look for a loud pair to complement the 95-cent shoes. Try on bowling shirts and hats made out of aluminum cans and crochet yarn. Go to the junk section where you'll find ceramic owls, four-foot golfing trophies, and framed class photos. Make your way to the used-book section and look for a book published during your birth year. Walk past the irons, eggbeaters, blenders, and cracked records to the mauve plaid couch where you and your friend can read your new book. If you get kicked off the furniture, do the dust test on their cardboard desks.

End your time by going to dinner in your new outfit. Instead of a tip, give the waitress a 25-cent trophy for being a good sport.

Telescope Tour Guide

Choose a few points of interest in your area that your friend might enjoy visiting—scenic overlooks, historical sites, tourist attractions, etc. Drive to each place and pull an inflatable boat from the trunk for your friend to stand in as she looks through the $1.39 telescope you bought at the toy store. (The boat has no real meaning but may be symbolic of Washington crossing the Delaware. If your friend likes Lincoln better, you can use a log cabin—the prop is for effect only.) While she looks, give her a description of the site in tour-guide fashion, mentioning as many obscure and meaningless facts as you can muster. If she isn't paying attention, you probably bought a kaleidoscope and she's fascinated by the colors.

Long-Term Memories

To help a friend remember a good time you've had together, give her a memento. Here are some ideas:

Where you went	What you might give	What not to give
restaurant	matchbook	entire place setting
amusement park	brochure	Ferris wheel
bowling alley	score pad	cocktail waitress
basketball game	ticket stub	backboard
zoo	small stuffed animal	large live animal
train trip	smashed penny	railroad-spike necklace
lake	skipping rock	gaggle of geese
carnival	old cotton candy	three-headed fat lady

Where Did This Come From?

How is your friend going to respond when he walks to the mailbox to receive his new subscription to *Dog Show Journal?* How about *Whittling Digest? African*

Water Sports? Order a subscription to a strange magazine and have the issues sent to your friend's house as a special and creative gift.

Hide and Search

Every time you go to your friend's home, hide some of his personal belongings. This will cause frantic searches when he realizes his things are missing. Empty his sock drawer into a large vase behind the front door. Hide the bars of soap under the sofa. Put rolls of toilet paper in the fish tank. This practical joke may bring late-night panic calls asking where you hid the nasal decongestant. (We must warn you that if you do this too often, you may not be welcomed inside—

and you may find your home isn't very comfortable when it's been burned to the ground.)

Can You Take a Message?

When you call a friend at the office and he's not in, you have three options:

1. Hang up (too rude).
2. Leave a normal message (too boring).
3. Disguise a message (now you're thinking).

Think how embarrassed your friend will be if he comes back to a fictitious message that he'll have to explain to the receptionist—or the entire office. By leaving your phone number, your friend will solve the mystery after he has explained his way out of trouble. Here are a few examples:

- "This is Dr. Smith's office calling; it's regarding the blood test. He needs to call us ASAP."
- "Please tell Cindy that Reverend Smith will be glad to perform her wedding ceremony."

- "Have her call Sergeant Smith. We'll need her for some more questions."

- "Yeah, this is Tim Smith from the Plaza Hotel. He seems to have removed the TV from his room, and we'd like to have it back."
- "Just calling to confirm her mud bath and massage appointment."
- "The cadaver she ordered is in."

Look at That Body

When you can't be with your buddy, the next best thing is for him to see your body . . . *huh?* Roll out a

large piece of construction paper and lie on it. Have someone trace the outline of your body. Draw call-out lines from the body parts and make comments. For example: *fingers*—highly flexible from lack of use in writing letters to friends living east of the Mississippi River; *knees*—worn out from too much praying that Janine would quit dating you and move out here and marry me.

4.

Making Friends in Strange Places

Telephone, Line One, Please

If you spot someone you'd like to meet but are nervous about a face-to-face introduction, you can play detective to find out her name.

(We could write an entire chapter on different name-finding ideas, but if we spoon-feed you everything, what feeling of accomplishment are you going to receive when you finally meet this person? None. So figure out your own way.)

Once you know her name, go to the pay phones and call the place you're at. When she picks up the phone you can begin your introduction.

(Sure, we could write this introduction dialogue for you. We could have you as the video repairman she never called, a glass-blowing instructor that heard about her cheeks, or a normal guy in the restaurant phone booth trying to show how creative he is. But again, what does that do for you? Right—nothing. If you don't take ownership of this idea, it will never work. Would you like us to help you dial the number? Maybe we can meet this girl for you and tell her we are the authors of a book on creative friendships and that the boring guy standing by the door would like to meet her and establish a friendship. Or what if we do the

looking, find a girl that would make a good friend, and send you a photo? Better yet, maybe we could send her. Come on, start taking some responsibility. But if you're really in a bind, we have written some dialogue for you on page 155. Help yourself.)

Meeting People in Elevators

Friendly Floor

When someone gets on the elevator, ask, "Which floor?" When he says, "Five, please," cry out, "Five! My best friend used to live on five!" Now burst into tears and tell him how you miss your best friend, Al, who was run over last August in an accident with an angry Alpaca animal during an advanced archaeological expedition in the Andes, actually around Andalgalá, Argentina.

If he gives you a consoling pat on the shoulder, sigh, "Al used to do that when I was sad—thanks." Now ask him for his name. If he gives it to you, reach out and shake his hand: "Nice to meet you, Phil; I'm Fred."

Now that you know each other, feel free to frankly

inform him that you're pleased to again have a fabulous friend on the fifth floor. Ask him to forgive and forget your former foolishness (though the fate of your feckless friend was fact and not fiction) and beg him to be your felicitator by phoning Friday for some flag football.

If he flatly refuses, forget about him. You don't need another fickle friend.

Cash Incentive

Get onto a crowded elevator. As soon as the door closes and everyone begins to stare at the numbers above the door, take out a stack of hundred-dollar bills and wave them in front of the floor numbers: "Okay, my name is Alex, and I'm your elevator monitor. If by

the time we come to your floor, you can give me the name and favorite cartoon character of everyone in this car, I'll give you $1,000. Now start talking."

Elevator Trivia

If you don't have $1,000 on you, then tell people they can get off only if they answer a trivia question. If you find a poor sport who puts a gun to your head and says she doesn't want to play, just give her an easy question and let her off—don't let her spoil everyone else's fun.

Name Drop

Climb through the escape hatch in the ceiling and cut the cable as you announce to the folks below you, "It looks like we'll be spending the rest of our lives together. Why don't we get to know each other?"

Bank Line Buddies

While standing in line at the bank, unclip one end of the velvet rope and reattach it to the belt loop of the

pair of trousers in front of you. If the person in the trousers steps up to the teller when a bank robber is walking by, she'll pull down all the poles, possibly tripping the robber. If this happens, tie up the robber with the velvet rope before he realizes what's happened. Now put one foot on the robber's back and introduce yourself to everyone who comes to thank you. You'll be a hero, and people will be more than happy to get to know you. If you try this method and everything works right except the bank robber never shows up, take your foot off the bank president, untie him, and offer to buy a new pair of trousers for the person in front of you.

Personal Classifieds

DIVORCED FEMALE wanting meaningful relationship with any man capable of carrying on a conversation longer than seven words. Send photo and one complete sentence.

TAKE IT FROM ME, THIS IDEA REALLY WORKS!

MY NAME'S TOM. I'm looking for a confident person, I think. I hate talking on the phone, and so please drop me a line, if you want.

FEMALE FRIEND WANTED. Not particular, but would prefer an Aleutian Eskimo, between 50 and 51 years old, 5'10", who speaks fluent Dutch: 555-5862.

Imaginary Friends

In the search for a perfect friend, some individuals actually *create* one. They invent imaginary friends who fulfill all the shortcomings of their flesh and blood friends. Here's a typical conversation with Rick and his imaginary friend, Dave.

"I took BUILD-A-BUDDY to a baseball game and didn't feel ostracized . . . my BUILD-A-BUDDY even caught a foul ball."

"I'm no longer ignored by men who travel in pairs. I'm now noticed because of my BUILD-A-BUDDY."

"I use my BUILD-A-BUDDY for the car pool lane—he saves me hours each day."

RICK.   I think she likes me—what do you think?

DAVE.   [*No response*]

RICK.   You think so? She sure seems like it . . . but sometimes I just can't read her—you know what I mean?

DAVE.   [*No response*]

RICK.   I feel the same way. Women have that ability to keep you hanging. But I'll know more after tonight. How do you like my new jacket?

GREAT TIE, RIGHT DAVE?

DAVE.   [*No response*]

RICK.   Yeah, I think my hair looks good too. I'm looking good tonight.

DAVE.   [*No response*]

RICK.   Why thanks . . . I don't know about the best-looking guy in the county. But I think I'm okay.

DAVE.   [*No response*]

RICK.   Strong? Well, maybe it's the weight lifting that's made me look so strong.

DAVE.   [*No response*]
RICK.   I don't know if I'd go that far to say I look like a total stud . . . you really think so, huh?
DAVE.   [*No response*]
RICK.   Well, thanks man.
DAVE.   [*No response*]
RICK.   You'll probably meet more women when you're with me.
DAVE.   [*No response*]
RICK.   Sure—I'll protect you if those guys start picking on you. I'll bounce those bums out of town—you can count on that!

[*Suddenly Rick's* Mom *yells from the hallway*]

MOM.   Rick! Hurry up and get out of the bathroom. Your piano lesson is in ten minutes! By the way, who are you talking to in there?
RICK.   [*No response*]

19 Ways to Meet People in a Bowling Alley

1. Run and slide, stomach first, on the freshly-oiled lanes.
2. Put your head in the ball-cleaning machine.
3. Take the maraschino cherries from the bar and stick them in bowling balls.
4. Press the reset button before someone bowls, causing the ball to ricochet into the electronic scoring device.
5. Throw the eight-pin into someone else's lane.
6. Break all the pencils.
7. Drop a sixteen-pound ball on your backswing.
8. Line the gutter with children from the nursery.
9. Use the bowlers to your left as your pins.
10. Fill the rental shoes with styling mousse.

Where NOT to Meet Friends

- Elementary school (grow up)
- Dark alley
- Light alley
- Used-car dealer's party
- Terrorist-training support group

- Emergency room
- Graveyard
- Mental hospital
- Nudist camp
- Plane (when it's going down)
- Telemarketing job
- Bank robbery
- 976 numbers
- Domino tumbling championship

- Overeater's potluck dinner
- Amway conventions
- On the set of a *Solid Gold* taping
- Magic shows (they'll disappear)
- Fabric shops
- Billiard parlor at 8:00 in the morning
- Dog obedience school
- Cleveland midnight film festival
- Rodeo
- Kmart shoe section
- All-night bar with blinking sign: GIRLS, GIRLS, GIRLS
- Yellow pages, under *escorts*
- Yellow pages, under *exterminators*
- Dump
- Family reunion
- Nerd convention (unless you're a nerd)
- Blood drive

HI... I NOTICED A LOT OF GIRLS AROUND HERE AND FIGURED IT MUST BE A GOOD PLACE TO MAKE FRIENDS.... I'M JILL!

11. Use the information phone line to order out for pizza.
12. Turn the video games to face one another so no one can play.
13. Ask for a tour of the snack bar.
14. Yell, "peanuts, popcorn, bowling supplies," as you walk through the crowd.
15. Write gossip about the management on the overhead scorer.
16. Volunteer to keep score for bowling leagues and cheat for the underdogs.

17. Jam the ball return with bowling shoes.
18. Buy bowling shirts at a thrift store and sell them in the parking lot.
19. Put baby powder in your hair and join the senior-citizen tour.

5.

Childish Friendships

If your childhood was like most, you had more friends in elementary school than at any other time in your life. What's the secret to friendships that made us so successful when we were little? We don't know either. But in case you'd like to recall those years in the hope of rediscovering it, here are some flashbacks you can use to venture back to your fourth-grade friendships.

A Flashback for Girls

Ask Sally if she'll be your best friend. If she says yes, tell her she's got to do something mean to Molly to prove it. If she says she doesn't want to be your best friend, tell her you hate her guts and that you heard Molly say she hates her too. If she cries, tell her that Molly makes *you* cry sometimes and you think that Molly is spoiled because she doesn't have to clean her room because her mom feels sorry for her and so Molly can do whatever she wants and doesn't get in trouble for it and doesn't even get in trouble when she says "I hate Sally" in front of her mom and hasn't even been spanked but she sure deserves it.

Then tell Sally that even though Molly hates her guts, you don't, and that you'll even erase her name if Molly writes it on the bathroom wall at school and puts bad words next to it. Now ask her again if she'd like to be your best friend. If she still says no, write

"S.P." on your hand and tell Sally it stands for "Sally protection," which means Sally's a dirty bird and people who play with her are dumb-dumbs and they better write "S.P." on their hands or they'll be dumb-dumbs too. Now go find Molly and start from the top, saying all the same things. At next recess, tell Molly that she's not your best friend anymore, and that Rebecca is.

The next day, ask Molly, Sally, and Rebecca to spend the night at your house on Friday night. Stay up all night and talk about Mariann, whom you didn't invite because she got elected class monitor by promising everyone free Girl Scout cookies because her mother is the Girl Scout troop leader. When your mom comes in at two in the morning and tells you to be quiet, pretend you're asleep. After she leaves the room, try with all your might to keep from giggling, but lose the battle and start everyone doing the same. Try to laugh into your pillow, but stop when you realize that it makes your giggle sound even funnier.

Finally, to get out the giggles, start to tell a ghost story. Right at the scariest part, when you have to go to the bathroom really bad and can't hold it any longer, leave everyone in the dark, go to the bathroom, slip the shower cap over your head, and leap back into the room to scare everyone. Tell Rebecca to stop crying because you were only joking.

When your mom comes in and asks you why you're still up and why Rebecca is crying, tell her that she must have had a bad dream. When your mother asks you what in the world you're doing wearing a shower cap, tell her that your head was cold. When Molly, who is pretending to be asleep, giggles at this last remark, throw your pillow at her and tell her to be quiet. When your mom leaves the room saying, "If you don't go to sleep this instant, I'll never let you have friends spend the night again," say you're sorry and that you'll be quiet now.

After she's gone, pretend to snore but start laughing again because Sally's snore sounds like Fred Flintstone's. Then whisper to each other about boys until six in the morning when you finally fall asleep.

A Flashback for Boys

Go over to Kyle's house—he's your best friend. Go into the backyard to look at the clubhouse his older brother, Rick, built with some friends. When Rick and his friends tell you you can't come inside because you're not members of the club, ask them how you and Kyle can join. They tell you that if you pass the initiation you can join, but to pass, you've got to go into Old Man Druey's garage, push the electric garage door closer, count "one-alligator-two-alligator-three-alligator," and run out before the door shuts on you.

After you and Kyle sneak into Old Man Druey's

garage, push the electric garage door closer, count "one-alligator-two-alligator-three-alligator," and run out just before the door shuts on you. Try to catch up to the older boys, who are laughing and skipping back to the clubhouse. When you finally catch up to them in the backyard, ask them if that means you're in the club now. When they say yes, shout, "Yea! We're in the club!" Rick and the other older kids smile and say, "We quit." Then Rick says, "Okay, we're starting a

30 YEARS LATER...

I'M AFRAID IT'S ALL VERY LEGAL, JASON, IT SEEMS THAT SINCE YOU NEVER LET MR. SMITH INTO YOUR CLUB, HE IS NOW GOING TO BUY YOU OUT AND RUN YOUR BUSINESS BANKRUPT...

new club: me, Bill, Rudy, and Jason are in it. No fourth graders allowed."

When Kyle goes into the house crying, go in with him and cry too. When Kyle's mother goes out and yells at Rick, you and Kyle watch from behind the curtain. When Rick comes in the house to say he's sorry and that they've changed the rules of the club to let fourth graders in, ask him if you can join this new club. When he tells you that to pass the new club's ini-

---

Conversation Flashback

FRIEND. You're not my friend anymore . . . you're . . . a . . . stupid idiot!

YOU. I know *you* are, but what am *I?*

FRIEND. Turn up your hearing aid—I said you were a stupid idiot.

YOU. I'm rubber and you're glue; whatever you say bounces off me and sticks to you.

FRIEND. So what?!

YOU. Why don't you just shut your trap!

FRIEND. Why don't you make me?!

YOU. I don't make trash; I burn it.

FRIEND. Then how come you're not on fire?

YOU. That was so funny I forgot to laugh.

FRIEND. Oh, real good come back!

YOU. You trying to pick a fight?

FRIEND. No, I don't pick on babies.

YOU. I'm not a baby.

FRIEND. Are too.

YOU. Am not.

FRIEND. Are too, are too!

YOU. Am not, am not!

FRIEND. Are too, are too, are too, to the millionth power!

YOU. Am not, am not, am not, to the zillionth power!

tiation you've got to smear mud all over your face and crawl backwards on your hands and knees down the street, tell him you'll do it only if he promises not to quit and make a new club as soon as you do it.

As soon as he promises, go out, smear mud all over your face, and crawl backwards down the street. When you're done with the initiation, go back to the clubhouse and start to go inside. When Rick and the other older kids say, "We quit. We're starting a new club," remind Rick that he promised not to. When he says that he's president and that he can do whatever he wants to, try to pull Kyle away from Rick's throat. When the older kids chase you out of the backyard, run all the way back to your house, sneak into your little sister's room, and pin her entire doll collection to the ceiling with thumbtacks.

Styles of Conflict Resolution

If a relationship is growing there will be tension. But if kids don't grow up, they never learn to deal with conflict until it's too late. We have researched four different age groups and discovered the following differences.

Age	First reaction to conflict	Action step toward resolution	What is usually said
6 months old	cry	cry	"Waa," "Aaa," or "Baa"
3 years old	cry	scream and cry	"Mommmmmmmy"
6 years old	anger	punch to the back or throw blocks	"I'm telling"
93 years old	doesn't notice	fall asleep	"Huh?"

6.

Etiquette

We've lost count of the number of letters sent to us from people desperate to become conversant in the international language of friendship—etiquette. Many of the letters betrayed a desperation in their authors. This sad note, scrawled on a Wal-Mart cafeteria napkin, typifies the hopelessness of many: "I want to be socially active, have friends, host parties, and be invited to other people's weddings and bar mitzvahs and Tupperware parties and funerals. But I don't know how to act—I'm a social Neanderthal." Good friendships require good etiquette, and if you don't have it, here's how to get it.

Step 1: *Think* Neat

Proper etiquette begins with the proper frame of mind: neat people *think* they're neat. Go to a mirror right now. Okay, now look yourself squarely in the eyes, and recite the Neat Thinker's Motto:

> *I am neat. I am normal. I am not*
> *a social Neanderthal.*

Now you've got to mean it, or this exercise won't work. Recite the Neat Thinker's Motto ten times:

I am neat. I am normal. I am not
a social Neanderthal.
I am neat. I am normal. I am not
a social Neanderthal.
I am neat. I am normal. I am not
a social Neanderthal.
I am neat. I am normal. I am not
a social Neanderthal.
I am neat. I am normal. I am not
a social Neanderthal.
I am neat. I am normal. I am not
a social Neanderthal.
I am neat. I am normal. I am not
a social Neanderthal.
I am neat. I am normal. I am not
a social Neanderthal.
I am neat. I am normal. I am not
a social Neanderthal.
I am neat. I am normal. I am not
a social Neanderthal.

Do you feel neat? You should, because you *are* neat. Wasn't that simple? Who knows, Princess Diana could be sending you a dinner-party invitation right now. But before you check your mail, you've got to complete step two.

Step 2: *Act* Neat

No matter how well mannered you *think* you are, others will not share your opinion if you embarrass them with an ignorance of all that is proper in dress, speech, and behavior. To educate you in this area, we've listed some rules of etiquette in an easy-to-read, question-and-answer format. By memorizing these essentials, you'll not only prevent social catastrophe, but establish yourself as a socialite of the high-

est order. There's a quiz at the end of the chapter to test your new knowledge.

I have several distinguished friends who like to socialize with me, yet I feel awkward when presenting them to others. Are there rules about who should be presented to whom first?

Presenting a friend to another friend is one of the main responsibilities of your friendship. Always present a person of lesser distinction *to* a person of greater distinction. For example, let's say that you'd like to introduce your cousin, the Emperor of Japan, to your best friend, Bud: "Your Excellency-Cousin, my best buddy, Bud; Bud, my cousin, His Excellency, the Emperor of Japan."

YOUR MAJESTY,
I WOULD LIKE TO INTRODUCE
MY BROTHER, THE EGG-SUCKING,
PIG-FACED, DOG-BREATHED
SLIMY COCKROACH.

YO.

Does age have a say in presenting someone to another?

Yes. Present someone younger *to* someone older. For example, if you're at a party in Foothe, introducing your young wife, Lady Ruth Boothe of Snoothe, to your personal friend and member of parliament from Goothe, the honorable Lord Hoothe, you'd say, "Lou Hoothe, Lady Boothe; Ruth, Lord Hoothe."

I never know what to do with my napkin. Do I leave it in my lap folded, or unfolded? When may I set it on the table again?

If you're using a small luncheon napkin, unfold it completely and put it in your lap. A dinner napkin is larger, and so you should leave it folded in half in your lap. If the host serves you a fitted bed sheet for a napkin, unfold it completely and fit the two bottom corners about your feet, the top two about your shoulders. Regardless of the size, never place it on the table again until everyone leaves the table after dinner. If you've used your napkin as a repository for any disgusting foods you've pretended to eat, empty the contents into a planter, pet, or purse.

When I have a dinner party, is it necessary to fold the napkins into cute shapes?

It isn't necessary to do so, but it's a great way of showing your guests that you have all the time in the world for such silly pursuits. Here are some of the more popular napkin shapes: fan, bouquet, castle, funnel, Sistine chapel, '59 Cadillac, Beatrice logo, Lucille Ball silhouette.

I've been to several dinner parties lately where a rude guest has virtually ruined the fun. What can I do to prevent this from happening?

If a fellow dinner-party guest becomes boisterous, use your napkin to silence him, but only if you can do so discreetly. If the offender is seated directly across from you, roll your napkin diagonally into a whip, dip the end into your water glass, and snap the weapon at his knees. If he's seated far away, "accidentally" drop a rock-hard dinner roll onto the napkin in your lap, grasp opposite sides of the napkin with your hands, and snap the napkin taut, sending the projectile to the target (be sure to keep your head back during the launch). If the disruptive person is seated next to you, wad the napkin into a ball and place it in his mouth.

I have a very weak digestion—all but the most mild foods cause me to burp. Must I excuse myself and leave the room every time I feel one coming on?

There's no need for you to feel ashamed or embarrassed about this problem. If you must burp, flaunt it. If people glare at you, point to the person next to you.

I had a rough childhood, and my therapist says that one of my ways of coping was to block out much of it. Unfortunately, one of the years I've blocked out is the one when I was taught how to eat with utensils. Eating with my hands wasn't much of a problem until I started getting invited out to dinner. Now when I go out, I have no clue as to which utensil to use when, and for what.

Don't let the dozen or so utensils lined up at a fancy place setting frighten you. Most of them are for show, left over from an era when silver was cheap. The safest thing to do if you feel embarrassed is to find your butter knife and use it exclusively. You can't go wrong with a butter knife.

But there must be some practical use for the other utensils?

There are three other uses, and all but the most cultured seem unaware of them. If your filet mignon is undercooked, you can silently notify your waiter by jabbing all the knives into it. If the conversation lulls, you can hang a teaspoon from your nose (if you see someone else do this, be polite and follow suit). If you slip silverware into a friend's coat pocket and pull it

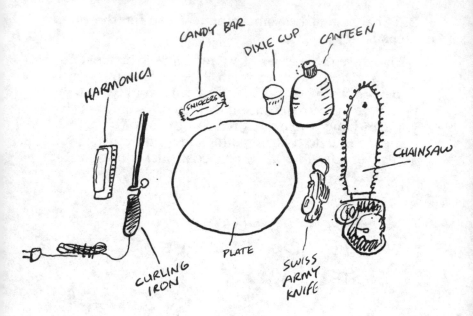

out just as he passes the maître d', you'll have taken part in some tasteful waggery.

I love throwing parties, but I have a difficult time dealing with certain guests who don't know when it's time to leave. How do I drop the hint without being rude?

Here are the most effective ways polite hosts and hostesses can inform their guests that it's time to go.

- "Gosh, would you just *look* at the time!"
- "Those of us who actually put on these parties for our freeloading friends have to get up early to work to pay for our generosity."
- "I remember when I was a kid, I used to make my parents stay up late just so I could."
- "Do you mind if I stayed at your house tonight? There's a bunch of jerks staying at mine and it doesn't look like they'll be leaving."

- "Get out of this house, you social Neanderthal!"

What is the difference between Continental and American styles of eating?

Continental style dictates that you hold the fork in your left hand, your knife in the right. The American style is the same for cutting the food, but to eat, you set down the knife and transfer your fork to the right hand. The significantly greater amount of exertion required in the American style accounts for America's superiority in fitness.

Are there any other acceptable styles of eating?

Yes. One other style, Atlantean, has found limited acceptability at some of the finer fishing lodges in Saskatchewan. A cross between Continental and American, Atlantean style requires the eater to cut the food with her spoon in her left hand, the can-opener blade of a Swiss army knife in her right. The eater puts the knife down, transfers the spoon to her right hand, and uses the seafood fork to load the spoon with food. She sets down the fork, transfers the spoon back to her left hand, flings the food over her shoulder, says, "The heck with it," and goes to McDonald's for a filet of fish sandwich.

Neatness Quiz

Take the following quiz to test how well you've learned the essentials of etiquette covered in this chapter.

1. You're introducing your fiance, Linus, to His Royal Highness, Prince Charles of England. How do you state your presentation?
   a. "Your Royal Highness, Linus Aquinas; Linus, His Royal Highness."

   b. "Chuck, Linus; Linus, Chuck."

   c. Don't say a thing—Linus doesn't have to meet *all* your old flames.

2. At a dinner party, the hostess has served you a double helping of her specialty, potato-and-liver-tots. After one bite you can't recall ever putting a more disgusting thing into your mouth. How do you dispose of the eleven morsels still on your plate?

   a. Hide them in your socks (or your neighbor's socks if you're not wearing any).

   b. Mold them into a table decoration.

   c. Cache them into your cheek and then excuse yourself for a journey to the bathroom.

Bad Etiquette

- When meeting girls for the first time, NEVER introduce your friend as a convict on a leave of absence.
- When visiting a wild animal park, NEVER use your automatic windows to lower the passenger's side.
- When parked behind a pack of Hell's Angels, NEVER honk the horn and duck.
- When fishing for shark, NEVER stuff your friend's pockets with live bait.
- When your friend is being robbed, NEVER tell the burglar that he has $100 hidden in his wallet.
- When your friend gets his car repossessed, NEVER ask for a ride to work.
- If your friend is upset over getting a bad haircut, NEVER ask how much she paid for it.

   d. Create a distraction (e.g., "Is that a mongoose playing with your Persian cat, Gwen?") and then drop the food into your napkin.

   e. Kick your neighbor in the shin and put them on her plate when she reaches down to rub the bruise.

3. Your third helping of paprika-and-raisin bisque doesn't agree with you, setting off a burping attack: What do you do?

   a. Carry on your conversation—people will just think your voice got lower.

   b. Each time you feel a burp coming on, make a louder noise to mask it: clap, slam the table,

---

• If your friend's dog dies, NEVER bark when you cough.

HEY, I HEAR SIT-UPS ARE REAL GOOD FOR A FLABBY TUMMY. 'COURSE I DON'T MIND. I LIKE PUDGY WOMEN!

drop a serving dish on the crystal, throw your plate on the floor.
c. After each burp, glare at the woman seated beside you and say, "Excuse *you!*"

4. You're a guest at a fabulous party hosted by your boss and her husband. It's after midnight, and it seems that you're the only guest remaining—the rest left about an hour ago. Your hostess is dozing off on the couch, the host has gone to bed. You should . . .
   a. Awaken her and ask for a raise.
   b. Awaken *him* and say goodnight.
   c. Go around the house and empty everyone's glass.
   d. Stay there as late as you want—it doesn't matter. You don't have a job to worry about anymore.

5. You're sitting at a table in a nice restaurant, looking down on a setting that includes four forks lined up to the left of the plate. From left to right, what are each of these forks used for?
   a. The first one is to be used until you drop it on the floor; the second until you accidentally fling it across the room while pointing out the woman in the purple hair; the third is used until you bend it prying off the cap of the relish jar you requested with your lobster; the fourth fork is the only one used for eating.
   b. Three are for the dieters who don't order anything but instead take "little" bites of your meal until there's nothing left; the fourth fork is for you to scrape up the remnants.
   c. Who cares—just order soup.

7.

Friends and Money

Mixing the two powerful forces of friends and money is a dangerous undertaking. Unfortunately, you can't avoid it. What you *can* avoid is some of the grief caused by the combination. Here are some helpful tips for doing so.

Using Your Friends as Tax Deductions

The new tax laws make it extremely difficult to take full financial advantage of your friendships. But there *are* a few loopholes left, and with proper planning, you can realize substantial tax savings. PLEASE NOTE: Each person's tax situation is unique; before claiming any of these deductions, consult a qualified tax accountant.

Dependents

Do you have a friend who's always hanging around your home, eating your food, running up your heating bill, making frequent operator-assisted calls to Islāmābād? This person is known as a dependent. Claim him.

Business Meals

Let's say that you're having lunch with a friend (Hilberto's in Santee, California, is a nice place) and you ask her, "How's your love life?" She glares at you, "None of your business!" You pursue it, "I'm making

103

it my business, Abigail, I'm concerned for you! Now tell me, how are you and Theophilus doing?" If your friend agrees to let you make this topic "your business," then your meal is a "business" meal. Write it off.

Profit and Loss

In a college accounting class you become friends with Bert, who one day introduces you to his uncle, the business tycoon. His uncle hires you when you graduate; in five years you work your way up to chief financial officer, making $225,000 a year plus bonuses.

Now let's say that instead of meeting Bert in your accounting class, the college computer made an error that caused you to take the class the following semester. So instead of meeting Bert, you meet Biff. He introduces you to *his* uncle, who hires you out of college. But his uncle turns out to be a business buffoon; after five years he drives the dying company into bank-

THIS COULD WORK!

ruptcy, and you're out of a job. Because you became friends with Biff instead of Bert, you miss out on $1 million in just a few years. In other words, Biff has become a financial liability. As such, you can claim the income you *didn't* make through Bert's friendship as a loss.

Medical Deduction

If the cost of medical treatment for the pain in the neck a friend causes you exceeds 6 percent of your Adjusted Gross Income, you may deduct the excess (but only if you itemize).

Deduction for Early IRA Distribution Made to Help a Friend Who Turns Out to Be an Idiot

This is a small loophole open to very few taxpayers, but if you're eligible, it's worth taking. Here's how it works.

If a friend sees a very clean, slightly used BMW for sale but doesn't have the guts to tell you the real reason she's asking you for $5,000 is to make the down payment, telling you instead that her aunt's dying wish is to see the Roy Rogers Museum in Victorville, California, and that she needs the money to fly her aunt round-trip from the Yukon before it's too late, and if you buy the story and make an IRA deduction before age 59½ (in essence, "unsheltering" the $5,000, which increases your income by that much, and permits the IRS to slap you with a 10 percent early distribution penalty), you may deduct the $5,000 as a loss and avoid the early distribution penalty—but only if you promise to write a note to your mother to inform her that she did, in fact, raise an idiot.

Lending Money to a Friend

Loaning money to a friend is a really good way to lose him. But if you have to do it, get him to sign a note something like this:

I, Fritz Muff, agree to repay my dear friend and buddy for life, Harold Burpstein, every penny of the $239 I borrowed from him on August 15, 1988. I further acknowledge his generosity and declare my sworn fealty to him by dismissing any thought of ever stiffing him, nay, never, spit in my eye, hope to die, nuh-uh, I wouldn't do it. No. And if I don't repay him within 60 earth days, I will voluntarily move to Mars and permit him to use my name to describe filthy things that only bad people mention.

Signature _____ *Date* _____

Borrowing Money from a Friend

If your friend gives you a note as proof of the money you owe her, be sure to read the fine print. Balloon payments, usury, and promises of first-born children are not uncommon and can put unnecessary strains on a friendship.

Who Pays for What?

Who buys when you go out with your friends? Do you go dutch? Does the winner always buy? Check out these little known paying facts.

Buying Gas for Your Car

You should buy when . . .
- You run two yellow lights, the make of your car has more than three vowels, and the combined weight of your passengers exceeds 3,000 pounds.
- Your hood release is automatic, your passenger has Swedish ancestry, and your tires are bald.
- The colors on your bumper sticker are to the left of the color wheel.
- You run out of gas while you're alone.
- You get the speed of your car to equal the score of your SAT test.

Your friends should buy when . . .
- Your passengers don't acknowledge your presence.
- Your wallet is full of tissue and your nose is bleeding.
- Your stereo is more important than your passengers.
- You have just bought lunch and paid for the concerts.
- Your car is used for a demolition fund raiser.

Buying Food

Fast food. The person who has the most zits, greasiest hair, and greatest fat content never has to pay for his food. That person needs to save his money for personal hygiene.

Fancy restaurant. Since everyone puts on an act to fit in at these restaurants, the person that buys is the first one to break the act. These acts might include:

Something to Think About

What if your friend Tim gave you four shares of Apple stock. You sold the shares and invested half the money in interest bearing CDs. With the other half of the money, you bought two purebred German shepherds for your friend Annette and a video game to put in Keith's 7–11 store.

Approximately 380 people enter Keith's store per day. One-fifteenth of those people play video games. Every week you collect an average of $160 in quarters.

With the money from the video games, you begin to pay for a tractor lawn mower from Sears. It takes six months to complete the purchase. During this time you realize that Annette's shepherds are pregnant—there's money to be made on her puppies. Meanwhile, you are paying Sam's little brother Eddie $6 an hour to mow lawns that you have contracted. He mows 30 lawns a week but only gets half-price when he mow friends' lawns.

On February 29 (leap year), your interest bearing CDs can be withdrawn. While you're at your bank, you hear that Eddie accidentally ran not holding open the door, tripping at the entrance, drooling while ordering, drinking from the flower vase, or applying butter with your finger.

Buying Cigarettes

Real cigarettes. No one should buy these—they're bad for your health. Don't be so stupid.

Candy cigarettes. These are difficult to find. The first one to spot them buys.

over the sleeping German shepherds at Annette's house. In your fear and frustration, you leave the bank quickly, dropping your money on the way out. On the way to Annette's you see Keith's store on fire—everything inside is destroyed. It's been a tough day. You're exhausted, but the question remains: how much actual money versus potential money did you lose, and what are the chances of this happening on the next leap day?

OH YEAH, THAT MAKES SENSE.

Buying Gatorade After a Game

Basketball. The losing team buys—if it's a half-court game, the drinks must be diet.

Baseball. In most cases the first baseman buys—he's usually big, dumb, and rich.

Golf. This sport doesn't involve sweat—there's no reason to drink.

Hockey. Since most hockey players don't have teeth, they prefer milkshakes.

Bad Opening Sentences for Trying to Borrow Money

- "Hey, Dipstick, can you advance me a few bills?"
- "Yo, Cheese Breath, can you float me some dough?"
- "Tightwad, do you think you can lay aside some of your squeaky cash?"
- "Miss Cellulite, what's the chance of your dishing out some bucks?"
- "Hey, Chicken Legs, how about lending from your surplus?"
- "I know you're a luxurious, stuck-up pig, but I'm sure you've got a few extra bucks you can loan me."
- "Hey, Mr. Lottery Winner, do you have some of that state-funded money available for loans?"

What to Do If Your Friend Has Forgotten to Pay You Back

It's difficult to remind a friend that he owes you money. He may have forgotten the loan, and he might be embarrassed if you ask for the payback. Following are a few ways to help you get your money:

- Borrow money from him and forget to repay it. If he asks for his money, remind him of the time he borrowed money from you. (It is considered inappropriate to charge interest, especially if you want to keep your friend.)
- Use subliminal dialogue while talking to him. Insert messages in nonrelated sentences. Talk quickly so he doesn't consciously notice what you're saying. For example, "Bob, it's good to see you. Did you happen to catch *(you owe me money)* the game last night? I had tickets *(don't forget the money you owe me)* right behind the dugout. Give me a call next week and I'll see if I can get us some *(money)* tickets."
- If subliminal dialogue is too difficult, you may want to try the popular subtle-hint approach. This is where you deliberately use key words to trigger his memory. For example, "Bob it's good to see you. I'd rather see you than all the **money** in the world. Did you **forget** to watch the game last night? I had to **pay back** an old friend, and so I got us tickets right behind the dugout. **Return** my call next week, and I'll see if I can **finance** some tickets."
- If you have an answering machine, tape this message: "I'm not in right now. I'm out looking for ways to earn some money. I've run into some financial difficulties, and I'm having trouble finding money."
- When you're with this person, "forget" to bring

your wallet into the movies, restaurant, or store so he is forced to pay for everything. Keep a record of what he spends until his outgo equals your payback. If he enjoys paying for you, stay absent-minded.

Investing with Friends

Since investing with friends is a sensitive subject, we have developed some rules of thumb to note before you risk a withdrawal.

1. Investing with someone who calls you "big guy," "buddy," or "my main man" is a no-no.
2. Investing in swampland or swampbush with swamp people merits a second thought.
3. Anything to do with the breeding of small farm animals is a bad investment.
4. If your friend has never before made a good in-

vestment but always claims "this is the one," stay away.

5. Investing during National Possum Week (usually the first week in October) has proven to be good.
6. People who consider fast food in the same class as gourmet should be shunned.
7. People who would vote for William "Refrigerator" Perry as one of the sexiest men in America are people with bad sense who don't make wise investments.
8. If you enjoy your friendship, stick to playing tennis together and leave investing for those who can afford to lose friends.

9. Investing with people who have more than four tax shelters and are looking for investments where a loss will be encouraged should be discouraged.

8.

Bad Friends

Oh, friendship is sweet.
　　Sometimes. But it can be nasty too. The source of some of your greatest joys is also the source of some of your most dangerous temptations.

The sad truth is that your friends are the ones most likely to lead you into behavior you know is wrong. The pressure to conform is greatest from those who are closest. Of course, when the pressure to do something we don't want to do becomes great, we're told to "just say no." We all know that, sometimes, it's a lot harder than that. Read the experience of Steven Huntflaaker (not his real name):

I told them yesterday, "NO!" But three of them called me last night and tried to talk me into it. "C'mon, Steve," Gilbert coaxed, "It's going to be great! We know you want to do it—so why all the fuss?"

After I got rid of him, Charlotte called and really put on the heat. "Aren't we good enough for you anymore? Then why don't you go through with it? It'll be like old times!"

Tanya was next. "What's wrong, Stevie, you're not chickening out, are you?"

After the third call I was sweating; my hands were shaking and I was desperate for a way out of the suffocating pressure I felt. Then they came.

*Banging on my door at five in the morning, drag-
ging me out of bed—I couldn't take it any longer.
"Yes."*

*No sooner had the words left my lips than I felt
the rush of coffee, too strong and too hot, pouring
down my throat. They shoved me into the backseat
of Gil's Dodge Aries. Charlotte was sitting next to
me, a smile on her face, Bushnell high-powered
binoculars about her neck, Audubon bird book in
her lap.*

*Another Saturday morning of bird-watching,
and I hate myself.*

Saying no to friends can be extremely difficult. But
there *are* ways to do it. Listed here are some of the
most common pressure situations you'll probably find
yourself in—and the most effective ways to get out of
them.

When you don't want to drink . . .
- "No thanks—drinking does strange things to me.
  Then I do strange things to other people, like
  throw up on their laps."
- "Drinking makes me feel strange. And since I al-
  ready *look* strange, I don't need to *feel* it."

**When you don't want to get in a car with someone
who's been drinking . . .**
- "I'm not going to get in the car with you, because
  if we crash, I'll be the one who gets killed. Then
  you'll have to live with the fact that you caused my
  death, and my parents will sue you for everything
  you'll ever make in your life. See how I'm looking
  out for you?"
- "If I end up dead, my roommate will get my
  stereo, and that's more than I can handle."

When you don't want the drug someone is offering . . .
- I'm on a special medication which, if combined

with other chemicals, will make me rip your face off."
- "My parents told me not to take drugs because it would adversely affect my future—they'll kill me."

When you don't want to smoke tobacco, marijuana, carrot sticks, or gym socks . . .
- "I can't. My uncle is the Surgeon General."
- "No thanks, I try not to do anything that would make me look macho."
- "No—it makes it hard for me to breathe."
- "I'm allergic to bad breath."
- "I only smoke when I'm on fire."

When you don't want to go grunion hunting . . .
- "I can't go hunting for grunion—somebody ate all my decoys."

When you're with a bunch of your friends and someone suggests that you all scrape your initials onto the side of a Minuteman missile with the edge of a Susan B. Anthony dollar your friend Marlene just happens to have hidden in her purse for a special occasion such as this . . .

- (Why not?)

When someone hands you an untied helium balloon and tells you to take a hit . . .

- "Last time I did that, the windows shattered."
- "If you do that long enough your voice will stay that way."

When your friend Bill calls you during Monday Night Football and asks if you'd be willing to join him in renouncing capitalism and moving to a collective in Siberia . . .

- *"Nyet."*
- "I can't, my savings bonds haven't matured yet."
- "Okay, but can we wait until after the Super Bowl?"

When they come for you—to go bird-watching (this one's for you, Steve) (not his real name) . . .

- Birds and I have a deal: I don't watch their mating habits, and they don't watch mine."

When your friends Gina, Mariann, and Corenne, are trying to convince you to have your arm tattooed with a picture of a pig in a tuxedo playing trombone . . .

- "No." (If you need another way to say it, just get the tattoo—you deserve it.)

Those responses are just fine for the situations listed, but what about all the situations where you don't have a snappy excuse memorized? The following exercise is designed for you. Read through this dialogue, saying no to each of your friend's ideas. This

will help you learn to say no in a way that is forceful, to the point, and final.

FRIEND: Let's go rob a bank.
YOU: No.

FRIEND: Okay, how about a liquor store?

YOU: No.

FRIEND: You're tough to please. Oh, I know, let's dart in front of rapidly moving cars on the expressway.

YOU: No.

FRIEND: Try to run down pedestrians?

YOU: No.

FRIEND: Teach stray cats to ride motorcycles?
YOU: No.
FRIEND: Paint our teeth black?
YOU: No.
FRIEND: Smoke Q-Tips?
YOU: No.
FRIEND: Tape killer-whale photos to the insides of pet-shop aquariums?
YOU: No.

Did you make it through the list, replying with a re-sounding no to each tempting idea? If you made it through this exercise without succumbing to the pressure, you can probably stand up to *anything*. Good for you.

One of the World's Worst Friends

Rod is twenty-five but hasn't experienced much of the world because he's been in jail for the past nineteen years. He has a complex personality that few are willing to take the time to understand, which makes him lonely. He's easily bothered, and really, it's not his fault that he accidentally killed his last three friends—they knew he didn't like to be teased about being so short. He's a nice guy once you get to know him.

Seven Characteristics of a Bad Friend

Though the words *bad* and *friend* seem like contradictions, there are some people who fit the following descriptions. Evaluate your friends by these characteristics so you won't be stupid with your next choice.

1. A bad friend forgets everything important. This friend stinks and is even on the borderline of being an acquaintance rather than a friend. This is the guy who looks over your shoulder while you're talking to him. He won't acknowledge your birthday and may even forget your name if you don't remind him. On the other hand, this is the same guy who wants to be around you at a party if you know more people than he does. Words to describe this person are found in any biological dictionary: leech, scum, slime, etc.

2. A bad friend doesn't notice changes. This guy wouldn't notice if your lips were removed. He is trapped in his own world and has no idea there is reality outside his existence. He'll squint his eyes to look as though he's going to notice a change, but when he can't figure it out within five seconds he'll shrug it off without further concern. He'll question your friendship and blame you for not caring if you don't notice the slightest change with him. What a jerk!

3. A bad friend makes you feel uncomfortable. When you're around this person you feel weird, unable to be yourself. It's a strange feeling, like when your underwear is too tight or when someone invades your personal space. It's not pleasant, and you don't ever want to repeat this experience. You can get more satisfaction from watching an educational movie than from being with this person.

4. A bad friend pulls you down. This person seems to bring out the worst in you. While you may seem to have fun, the end result is compromise in important areas of your life. Afterwards, you're usually upset because he had this negative influence. You promise yourself that you're going to reverse things next time and be a constructive influence on him. But the same thing happens time after time. We suggest that you stay away from this person, throw up on yourself, and yell "bad friend, bad friend" when you're about to give in to temptation.

5. A bad friend puts you down. This is the person who is always making fun of you. She will put you down simply because she has the "skill" to use her tongue negatively. She will laugh at the "wit" of her verbal assault while you crumble on the inside. The next time your friend's mouth gets out of hand, try using Scotchguard, pliers, dog drool, or sandpaper. Just don't say anything while you do it—you wouldn't want to lower yourself to her level.

6. A bad friend is nowhere to be found in time of need. A bad friend won't come around because she doesn't care about you. You call her before she calls you. She is too busy watching "I Love Lucy" reruns to be with you. Just make sure this person isn't your swimming "buddy" in lifesaving class.

7. A bad friend doesn't want to be seen with you. When your implied friend never wants to be seen with you, it's a good indication that he can't stand you. There must be some depth to your friendship or he wouldn't be at your house, and so at least you've got that going for you. But if you want to go out of the house with someone who likes you, get a new friend or buy a dog.

9.

Good Friends

You Know You Have a Good Friend When . . .

The proof of a good friend lies not in his strengths, but in his tolerance of your weaknesses.

- She cares more about you than her money.
- He allows you to ride in the front seat.
- She holds the toilet seat as you throw up.
- He sticks up for you—even when it's your fault.
- She doesn't make fun of your singing.
- He helps you move without your asking.
- She isn't grossed out by your acne.
- He warns you of your bad breath.

THE GUY BEHIND ME
IS VERY SENSITIVE ABOUT
HIS EARLOBE SURGERY,
WHATEVER YOU DO,
DON'T LAUGH AT HIM...

TOLL

- He doesn't take out your "ex" even though she has a crush on him.
- She takes the blame for something you did.
- She lets you kill the wasp on her neck.

- She washes your car on a rainy day.
- He fights the mountain lion that was chasing you.
- She pulls off the bloody tissue left on your face from shaving.
- In the locker room, he lets you use the last of his deodorant.
- She drives you places and doesn't ask for gas money.
- He eats your vegetables so you can have dessert.

- She lets you in her club without going through the initiation.
- He acts as the lookout as you go to the bathroom.

Eight Characteristics of a Good Friend

Good friends are rare! They are a source of continual blessing and encouragement. We have outlined eight qualities of a good friend. Let your friend know where he or she is hitting the mark. Then evaluate yourself and make an assessment on your caliber as a friend.

1. A good friend remembers important dates. We have days that are important to us. Acquaintances remember birthdays, but good friends remember significant anniversaries. These might include the time you got busted by the police, the day you watched a soap

opera without getting sick, the date of your first kiss, the week your hamster learned to use his training wheel, or the night you put small fish heads in the ice cube tray. It's nice when someone shares these with you.

2. A good friend allows you to be yourself. It's a comfort to take off your mask around friends and be the person you were created to be. Being real is one of life's greatest gifts. Around good friends you can eat like a pig, smell like you want, share your worst sins, say what you think, make fun of yourself, and trip over your own feet without feeling embarrassed.

3. A good friend notices subtle changes. It's nice when someone notices your haircut (unless it was the result of a biking accident) or notices you've shed ten pounds. A good friend not only notices changes but points them out. She is positive when she expresses her observations. You will never catch a good friend saying, "You look more like a hippo than a whale these days." (*See* Bad Friends)

4. A good friend challenges you to be your best. Because a good friend cares, he will challenge you to be a better person. It's not easy to get away with bad things. A person who doesn't care won't take the time to help you change. A good friend will tell you when you act stupid (unless you're writing a book); he'll point out that you hurt someone's feelings when you

asked to grease your frying pan with the moisture from his hair; he'll inform you of the food on your teeth as he hits you on the back of your head to dislodge the "thing" hanging from your moustache.

5. A good friend doesn't put you down. Being put down to build someone up at your expense hurts. A good friend looks for opportunities to make you look good—he'd never trip you in front of a girlfriend, pull down your shorts while you're speaking in front of a group of people, or drop a gallon of latex paint on your head before a job interview.

6. A good friend supports you in time of need. We all have times of need, times when support is a great gift. A friend's support communicates belief in you as a person.

Some people confuse concern with support. When they are concerned they may run to your rescue with cookies, an encouraging poem, or a piece of leftover cake. These are nice actions, but they aren't what you really need. What you *really* need is money—and if you had money you could buy your own cake.

7. A good friend wants to spend time with you. No one enjoys spending time with geeks, iguanas, spiders,

thieves, social deviants, boogymen, obnoxious children, or reporters. Once you prove you're not a member of one of those horrible, gross, nasty, tasteless,
and rude species, a friend should want to spend time
with you. When she finds out you're not perfect, a
good friend will accept you for who you are and enjoy
spending time with you.

   8. A good friend compliments you. We all love compliments. *(Why, thank you, we enjoyed writing it.*

That's really nice of you to think that, but we must continue. I hope you don't think we were fishing for compliments. We do admit it feels good to know you think this is the best book you've ever read.) Good friends take the time to compliment one another. When was the last time you paid compliments to your friends? Don't think they already know what you like about them—they don't. Your friends are dumb and need to be told. Go ahead, make their day. *(Thanks again on the nice words about the book. We hope you'll tell a friend.)*

10.

Romantic Friendships

Picnics

There's the traditional picnic: grassy park, holding hands, checkered table cloth, wicker basket, and ants. Then there's the nontraditional picnic for those ready for something new. Some ideas:

Pirate picnic. Eat in a cave, wear black, and feed each other with swords. (This can also double for a punk-rock picnic.)

THIS SUNSET PICNIC-AT-SEA HAS BEEN A GREAT IDEA. YOU DID BRING THE PADDLE, DIDN'T YOU?

Lost-at-sea picnic. Eat in an inflatable boat on a pool or pond. Wear blindfolds so you don't know where you are.

Airline picnic. Eat in the middle of a runway. Wrap your food in cellophane and include something no one would ever eat.

Space picnic. Eat dried food and drink Tang while your car is parked in the closed garage. Put your TV on

Do's and Don'ts of Setting Someone Up

Do

Make sure he isn't married.
Introduce him to "good" people.
Inform him if something is hanging from his nose.
Offer to buy *Creative Dating* and *More Creative Dating* to help him with date ideas.
Make sure he doesn't have any communicable disease.
Convince him he will have a good time.
Get excited when you tell him about her.
Point out his positive features.
Bring attention to his good qualities.

Don't

Set him up with your mother.
Say, "He's got a great personality."
Mention the word *marriage*.
Laugh while you're introducing him.
Act like it won't work out.
Try to match IQ's.
Point out hickeys.
Burst out laughing when she rejects him.

the hood, watch *Star Wars*, and steer clear of Darth Vader.

Phobic picnic. Drive around all day and eat nothing while talking about the different phobias that keep you from doing everything.

Dust picnic. Sit in a dirt field on a windy day and have your friends drive in circles while you try to eat.

Insect picnic. Lay your food on the grass and try to

Use the word "mediocre."
Point out past failures.
Mention the price of his clothes.

identify the different types of insects that consume your food.

Baby picnic. Eat in a crib. Throw food against the walls. Take things off the other person's plate and cry when you don't get your way.

"D" picnic. Plan all your actions to begin with the letter *D. D*abble in your food, *d*angle your feet in the stream, *d*ecorate the picnic area, *d*raw pictures of each other, *d*ig for worms, *d*elay going home.

11.

52 Ways to Show a Friend You Care

1. Give him $175,000 for his birthday.
2. Give his dog a bath. (If the dog already owns a bath, give it a Jacuzzi.)
3. Clean out her refrigerator, throwing out everything that expired in the Renaissance.
4. Wax her car.
5. Give him one of our books.
6. Make her something to eat. If she gets sick, comfort her with Pepto-Bismol.
7. Squeeze the acne on his back.
8. Fill the mailbox with flowers.
9. Leave an encouraging note on the inside of his tie.
10. Teach him karate.
11. Give her a back rub.
12. If your friend's car is scratched, sandblast the rest of the paint so she won't notice the scratch.
13. Leave a message on her phone recorder.
14. Treat her to ice cream.
15. Replant her garden.
16. Do her chores.
17. Pay his phone bill. (You'll be a better friend if you pay his mortgage.)
18. Start a fire for her to come home to. (Preferably in the fireplace.)
19. Scrub his radioactive pajamas.
20. Bet him on something you know you'll lose on.

21. Send him a lottery ticket. (With the condition that he'll share if it's a winner.)
22. Send her a tape of your ten best jokes.
23. Read her a fairy tale.
24. Do something clumsy to make her feel coordinated.
25. Buy him a museum.
26. Put a live animal in her cupboard.
27. Brush the fuzz on her favorite stuffed animal.
28. Applaud when she walks through the door.

29. Explain the difference between wrestling and rasslin'.
30. Create a new perfume and give it your friend's name.
31. Buy her a pillow and let her take a short snooze.
32. Plan a minivacation.
33. Arrange for an old friend to fly into town on his birthday.
34. Videotape four weeks of his favorite comedy.
35. Wax his skis.
36. Write a song.
37. Buy her a coloring book and crayons.
38. Leave a gift certificate for a candy store.
39. Buy him a best-seller.

40. Go shopping with her without complaining.
41. Fill a shoe box with pistachios.
42. Buy him an exercise video.
43. Get a price-quote for a coffin.
44. Make him a lint remover for his belly button.
45. Print his name on his golf balls.
46. Pick up the dog waste in her backyard.

47. Get her film developed.
48. Give her glass-blowing lessons.
49. Photocopy your face and leave it on her car window.
50. Pretend you're intelligent.
51. Paint her house. (Permission optional.)
52. Sharpen his pencils.

12.

Rating Your Friendships

It's time to take a close and serious look at your friendships. The following quizzes and charts will help you to determine the quality, depth, maturity, and strength of your relationships.

How to Tell If a Friend Doesn't Like You

1. Does your friend avoid returning your phone calls for months at a time?
2. Does she encourage you to take up hobbies like cliff diving, cobra training, or chainsaw juggling?

GET OUTA MY LIFE!

MAYBE I SHOULD CALL YOU LATER.

3. When you tell him your deepest secrets, does he write them down?
4. When you go out for a meal, does she insist you take separate cars and eat at different restaurants?
5. Have you had at least three close calls since you agreed to name him as sole beneficiary on your life-insurance policy?

If you answered yes to any of these questions, it could mean that your friendship is not what it used to be. You have two choices: (1) dump the bum, or (2) go back through the book and plan some outrageously good times to win your friend back.

The Fields-Temple Relationship Hierarchy

Through extensive study on the subject of friendship, we've discovered several amazing facts.

As a human being, you are simultaneously involved in twelve separate and distinct levels of nonfamily relationships. Every other human being on earth (excluding your family) fits into one of *your* relationship levels.

There is an inverse relationship between the quality and quantity of relationships you have at that level. In other words, as the quality increases, the quantity of persons with whom you relate at that level decreases. When shown diagrammatically, this inverse correlation forms an inverted triangle: the superficial levels of quality (and greater number of relationships) form the upper, wide portion of the triangle; the deeper levels of quality (and fewer number of relationships) form the lower, narrow portion of the triangle.

Every relationship starts out at the widest level. Some never progress deeper; others grow in quality and move deeper into the relationship triangle.

These twelve relationship levels and their correlation are shown in *diagram 58-b/341.*

DIAGRAM 58-B/341
THE FIELDS-TEMPLE RELATIONSHIP HIERARCHY

1. All the people who received a Publishers's Clearing House Sweepstakes "lucky bonus number"

2. Complete strangers

3. Those who have cut in front of you while driving

4. Those who have stood in line with you at the Motor Vehicle Department

5. Those who have promised to pay you back the money you lent them

6. Acquaintances

7. Those who say they're your friends

8. Those who have actually *paid back* the money you lent them

9. Friends

10. Close friends

11. Best friends

12. Buddies for life

Is Your Friend a Loser?

Occupation is a poor indicator of a person's character; however, a few lines of work are known to attract the kinds of people who happen to make poor choices for good friends. If you have a friend whose profession is one of the following, know beyond a shadow of a

doubt that he or she is a loser: Bank Robber, Drug
Dealer, Cattle Rustler, Terrorist.

Now that you know your friend the terrorist is a
loser, maybe it's time to review chapter 4.

Styles of Friendship

It's no secret that we treat friends differently as a
result of our diverse natures. Since we are also selfish,
we have different motives for being attracted to and
wanting friends. In our extensive research on the subject of friendships, we have discovered that people fit
into four categories. There are no exceptions to this

rule. Like it or not, you're one of four. We have affectionately identified each category with an animal.

The understanding that there are two broad styles of interacting with friends formed the basis for our research. Style one shows interest in individuals. This style indicates the regard in which people hold others—whether high or low—to care for, appreciate, love, enjoy, and show concern for individuals.

Style two measures the concern for depth in relationships—whether high or low—to know others on deep, emotional levels. Style two deals with transparency, secrets, past sins and failures—knowledge of what others are thinking and feeling is the ultimate satisfaction.

We found these two styles aren't extremes, rather they are different dimensions that work together to

complement friendships. These two styles comprise the four animal types. They are (1) *Teddy Bear*, high regard for the person with low concern for depth; (2) *Mole*, low regard for the person with low concern for depth; (3) *Fox*, low regard for the person with high concern for depth; and (4) *Fish*, high regard for the person with high concern for depth.

Teddy Bear

The intent of the Teddy Bear style is to maintain relationships at all costs. This person will deny or avoid conflict, or both, whenever possible. Basically, the Teddy Bear has no spine and is interested in a self-

---

Things You Should Know About Your Friends . . . Just in Case

Name: _____

Address: _____

Phone: (h) _____

       (w)_____

Birth date: _____

Special occasions: _____

Spouse's name (if married): _____

Children's names: _____

Favorite restaurant: _____

Favorite food: _____

Favorite movies: _____

Favorite sports: _____

Favorite color: _____

Gift ideas: _____

---

serving relationship rather than one dealing with reality and truth. He is so self-conscious that if anything goes wrong, he considers it his fault. The Teddy Bear will wallow on his stomach asking for forgiveness for things that weren't his fault. He's happy to cuddle, hug, sit, and talk. He is a supportive but draining friend who never leaves your house. If you want to end a relationship with a Teddy Bear, make him feel guilty. After a while he won't be able to handle the strain and will begin to hibernate.

Mole

The Mole is considered the "scum under the earth."

What he or she looks for in a date (if unmarried):

_____

Ideas for a surprise: _____

_____

He or she hates it when: _____

_____

What he or she takes pride in: _____

_____

Pet peeves: _____

Special awards received: _____

Bad habits: _____

Exotic fantasies (if it's any of your business): _____

_____

What would embarrass him or her: _____

_____

_____

He doesn't like people and cares less if others like him. Life for the mole is boring—he has no one to play with. The Teddy Bear would be a friend if the Mole would only talk and go to the Teddy Bear's house for dinner.

Fox

The Fox has to be "in the know." He isn't as concerned with knowing others as individuals so much as he is with knowing everything about them. The Fox uses his concern for depth in order to gather knowledge about others to persuade, gossip, and manipulate. The Teddy Bear and the Mole frustrate the Fox because neither wants to reveal much of himself. The Fox chases his own tail because he can't get the Fish out of the deep water—and the Fox hates getting wet. A wet Fox resembles a large Mole, and nobody likes a Mole.

Fish

The Fish likes depth and others—that's why they go deep, stay down long, and swim in schools. The Teddy

Bear and the Fish could be good friends—but the Bear usually ends up eating the Fish, which isn't usually good for relationships.

What Kind of Friend Are You Looking For?

By taking the following test you'll have a better idea of what type of friend you are looking for. Circle your answer in each category, add your points, and read the fitting description.

BODY

athletic	100 points
average	50 points
pudgy	25 points
fat	− 10 points

LOOKS

attractive	100 points
pretty cute	50 points
okay	25 points
dog	− 10 points

PERSONALITY

fun, outgoing, popular	100 points
gets along well with others	50 points
can carry on a conversation	25 points
step above mole in the food chain	− 10 points

HOBBIES

enjoys sports, fast cars, modeling	100 points
works well with hands	50 points
collects stamps and coins	25 points
collects scabs	− 10 points

IQ

180	100 points
160	50 points
120	25 points
80	− 10 points

SALARY

$100,000+ year	100 points
$24,001–$30,000	50 points
$12,000–$24,000	25 points
minimum wage	−10 points

CAR

Porsche	100 points
Honda	50 points
VW Bug	25 points
Yugo	−10 points

GOALS

to be cute, fun, popular and rich	100 points
to buy a house	50 points
to buy a Honda	25 points
to watch a movie without falling asleep	−10 points

Scoring System

500 to 800   You egotistical brat. Are you always concerned with wanting the best for yourself? Do you think your life is based on how other people observe you? You'd better reevaluate who you are and what you want with your life—you're headed in the wrong direction.

250 to 499   You'd better feel a little nervous after reading the above description—you're almost as bad. If you were better looking, you would probably want the best of everything. Chances are you're a seven on a scale of ten and you look at life through your number-seven lenses instead of the rosy-colored ones the pigs above use. Watch it buster—you're heading for trouble.

1 to 249   How does it feel to be incredibly average? You're probably the type who wears cords and shops for sales. Maybe you should try to add a little excitement to your life— how about Twinkies in a plain wrapper? If you're tired of people referring to you as mediocre, spend a few bucks on a self-help book!

−80 to 0   Get a job, a life, and a little initiative. This isn't high school any more. This is called *life*, and when the phone to reality rings you'd better answer it. Get some expectations. People judge the book by the cover, and if you've scored this low, our guess is that you're ugly.